Release It

Chrystle Browne

BookLeaf
Publishing

India | USA | UK

Presentation by *BookLeaf Publishing*

Web: www.bookleafpub.com

E-mail: info@bookleafpub.com

ISBN: 9789363302877

First edition 2024

For my children Tyler, Madison, and Israel. You can do all things.

PREFACE

This book of poems is meant to show that we all go through things that can either make or break us but changing our perspective and the people around us can make a huge difference.

You

Hey, you, yes, you are right there.
You matter, and you are enough.
You are doing your thing.
So keep making yourself proud.
Don't mind the naysayers and those who follow
the crowd.
Be yourself, and all things will fall into place.
The voices will whisper and make you
second-guess yourself,
But you stand up tall and let them know
You are Enough, flaws and all.

Mirror

Staring back at me, I see someone different.
The eyes tell a story of pain, defeat, and chaos.
The tears roll down my cheek. It's
warm to the touch, and it's cutting deep.
Memories, lies, and deceit:
Why can't I just look and see who I used to be?
Positive, Carefree, and Happy as can be.
What has the world done to me for this to be the
new me?

Affirm Yourself

Hello, beautiful people.
Yes, that means you too.
Pick your head up and learn to affirm yourself.
Turn the negative thoughts into positive ones.
 Learn to accept your flaws and have a ball.
 When you do good things and don't get that
round of applause, a pat on the back, or an Oh
Girl, you did That!
Clap for you and affirm yourself.
Sometimes, our biggest enemy is within, but
look in that mirror and learn to Win. Affirm
Yourself.

Taken

Taken
This movie shows as I waited for them to take
you
Out of my womb,
Cold air, drilling sounds, and one other patient
waiting.
The sounds, the thoughts, the fear in my heart.
The choice to play a film of a man searching for
his daughter, the feeling of what if.
The thoughts of you being my little girl
Venturing through this thing we call life
They called my name, and it was my turn to go.
As I wiped away my tears, I knew I would never
know your face.

3

My womb has carried three, but only two are
living.
It was not my decision, but the elders thought it
was not my time.
It was short-lived because, in a matter of time, it
was five months later when I saw those two
lines. Again, it was
a positive test, and I knew it was a sign
that my life had turned upside down, and I was
out of my home.
I was all on my own with hope and a dream to
make it on my own.
The unborn fetus was taking every bit of energy.
Numerous amounts of hospital visits.
Bedrest and maternity leave before I was even
12 weeks along.
I was only getting a percentage of my pay.
No way was I going to allow this to stop me
from being the best mom I could be.
I enrolled back in school eight months in.
There was no way I wasn't making it.
Every single doubt and question ever asked, all
the things they said I couldn't do, I surpassed.
I gave birth on a Wednesday and Saturday and
went back to class.

That alone was the reason I lost my room in the
shelter.
They wanted me to heal and lay low for a while.
No one was paying my fees, so that break was
not okay with me.
I was back to square one and had no choice but
to return home.
I grew up, and it pushed me to focus on my
baby.
You ask about his father.
We are still good friends and can talk about
anything.
During our 30-minute call, he wanders around
his four walls,
living in a cell because he wants easy money.
Nothing about this is funny, but he made
hundreds of thousands, which never changed
him.
He gave all his time to his 2nd born when he
was around.
Yup, my boy should've been number one, but
infidelity came around and knocked us. I didn't
know what to do or say because I had to guess
who already had a baby on the way.

D day

It was Love, or so I thought.
We said, "I do," and wanted to make it quick.
On the same day of his birth,
We went and vowed never to let go.
Until death does us part.
No one said that would be the day it was the
death of me.
I gave my all and loved wholeheartedly.
 I birthed a baby girl into this world.
I tried to make it work, but you were not ready
to fulfill the dad role.
Let's rewind to the start.
2009 was the year I worked for the Bullseye,
and
I became the target of his eye.
He said he knew from first sight I would be his
wife.
It wasn't all bad, but it was broken- beyond
repair.
It was Love, or so I thought.

Love

Love,
I love our Love no matter how crazy.
I love the laughs and the inside jokes;
I love just laying in complete silence.
I love the wrongs and the rights and everything
in between.
I love the cuddles and booger licks; no matter
how gross,
I love the realness and the opportunity for it just
to be.
The only thing we share for eternity.
I love the friction and static that forces us to
grow.
We work through it all no matter how hard we
hit the wall.
We always reverse and bring it back to reality.
I love that we will conquer it all.

T.M.I

T.M.I
My heart is in human form.
I can and will always choose success because
There are no words to express the joy, Love, and
kindness exuded through.
Thank you for choosing me.
Thank you for teaching me as I got to teach you
 and motivating and loving me when I didn't
know how to love myself.
You all are my forever, and it gets no better.
Continue to be the best version of yourself to
make this world great.
I am always proud and will be here through it
all.
Tyler Madi and Israel, everything I do is for you.

Giggles

To be young again
To live so carefree
No bills, no rules, just running free.
Giggles, bubbles, and hopscotch on the street.
Chalk all over the ground as you hop on the
beat.
Double Dutch bike ride:
You were rushing home to beat the street
lights—free minutes. After 9, an AIM message
full of everything you did and pics in your
favorite outfit. The song of the day and mood set
in your status.
Oh, what a life it was before social media swept
in and rocked us.

Self

Learning who I am and what I like was a
journey.
Therapy, yoga, boxing, and poetry were all
things I used to cope with when I felt like my
back was against the ropes.
Figuring out who I was before I became a mom
or a wife.
A journey that evolves each day as I rediscover
C.M.A.

Blanket

You are like a weighted blanket.
You ease anxiety, keep us warm and safe from
this reality, embrace our entire being, and love
unconditionally.
My heart smiles, and I'm all warm inside. I
always know that you choose me.
Your Love flows like a river, your words linger,
and you fill the voids.
You make me whole and new every day. I'm
grateful for your warm embrace.
Thank you for your spirit and for being the
living word.

Leave the Door Open

Leave the Door open like Bruno Mars.
Allow the Lord to do HIs thing.
He loves you through everything and is waiting
for you to let HIm in.
He is always around and wants to take over.
So push aside all the doubt and give him a shout.
A shout of praise and acceptance:
He created you, and you are wonderfully made.
He is calling you by name.
Allow room for the breakthrough; let Him work
through you.
He is faithful and loyal and will fight the battles
you don't see. So just leave the Door open and
let him through.

Home

Home
is not a place but more of a feeling only you can
give.
You can give it your all and keep it safe.
Safe in your arms, your Love is an ocean of
calm waves carrying away the worries—the
Worries that rattle your mind as you overthink.
Self-sabotage because we could have been great.

Middleman

The middleman
is always in the middle, having to play the fence.
Don't choose a side.
Remain neutral.
Keep things calm and copacetic.
But the real issue becomes your life.
They cause disarray, chaos, and confusion. A
head full of tales you cannot tell.
Keep everything in so you don't lose a friend.
Is this the life you have chosen?
Who is there to hear your side?
Who is there to calm your storm?
Who is coming to stand ten toes behind you?

Control

Control
Loose lips
Arguments
Hurtful words
Arguments
Physical, mental, and spiritual
abuse.
You are the only person in control of you.
Nothing and no one should get you out of
character because you are the only person in
control of you.

Listen

To the words you speak that cut so deep.
They are like vinegar to the lips.
They burn, sting, and hurt after too much
spewing.
Hurtful, Manipulative, and condescending, just
to name a few.
It all happens so fast, and you regret it the next
day.
You always have something to say, but you
should listen.

Let Me

You make it hard for me to love on you. So
consumed with what to and what not to do. You
have my heart, it's wide open.
I'm doing all I can to help you see, that this right
here can last an eternity.
Let's make it happen, change that me and you to
us and we.
There is no place left to go, but up
You came ready for war
Applying pressure, and got me to fall- for you
and everything you do.
Now I am here, and you are pushing me away.
I am really a whole vibe and your favorite place
to dine.
No regrets no doubts no drama pull up every
time and you know I'm right behind ya.
We can do this forever thing just open your heart
No need to be guarded and scared
We are locked in, keep riding this frequency.
Come here and let me show you why you only
need me.

This Far

You made it this far
Nothing can stop you.
You have survived everything that was meant to
rock you.
Keep being light and living according to your
purpose.
People come and go, but don't take it personally.
They are not meant to share your greatness but
to teach you a lesson.
Your heart is so big, and you have no fear
because God is on your side, and you will
continue to shine.
Please don't change, and never give up on
yourself.
You are the only person who has been with you
and never departed.
Love yourself first and stand firm on your
beliefs
because you have made it this far; no one can
take that from you.

www.ingramcontent.com/pod-product-compliance
Lightning Source LLC
Chambersburg PA
CBHW071255140726
47996CB00007B/2848